W9-DEW-985

Skip Count by 2, Now Can You?

Tracy Kompelien

Consulting Editors, Diane Craig, M.A./Reading Specialist
and Susan Kosel, M.A. Education

ABDO
Publishing Company

Published by ABDO Publishing Company, 4940 Viking Drive, Edina, Minnesota 55435.

Printed in the United States.

Credits
Edited by: Pam Price
Curriculum Coordinator: Nancy Tuminelly
Cover and Interior Design and Production: Mighty Media
Photo Credits: AbleStock, ShutterStock, Wewerka Photography

Library of Congress Cataloging-in-Publication Data

Kompelien, Tracy, 1975-
    Skip count by 2, now can you? / Tracy Kompelien.
      p. cm. -- (Math made fun)
    ISBN 10 1-59928-545-2 (hardcover)
    ISBN 10 1-59928-546-0 (paperback)

    ISBN 13 978-1-59928-545-0 (hardcover)
    ISBN 13 978-1-59928-546-7 (paperback)
    1. Multiplication--Juvenile literature. 2. Counting--Juvenile literature. I. Title. II. Title: Skip count by two, now can you? III. Series.

    QA115.K6648 2007
    513.2'13--dc22

                                                        2006017376

SandCastle Level: Transitional

SandCastle™ books are created by a professional team of educators, reading specialists, and content developers around five essential components—phonemic awareness, phonics, vocabulary, text comprehension, and fluency—to assist young readers as they develop reading skills and strategies and increase their general knowledge. All books are written, reviewed, and leveled for guided reading, early reading intervention, and Accelerated Reader® programs for use in shared, guided, and independent reading and writing activities to support a balanced approach to literacy instruction. The SandCastle™ series has four levels that correspond to early literacy development. The levels help teachers and parents select appropriate books for young readers.

Emerging Readers
(no flags)

Beginning Readers
(1 flag)

Transitional Readers
(2 flags)

Fluent Readers
(3 flags)

These levels are meant only as a guide. All levels are subject to change.

To skip count by 2

is to count in groups of 2. That means you skip every other number while counting.

Words used when skip counting:
every other
group
number
pair
twins

Here is a pair of .

The two are twins.

Here are two .

This is a pair of .

The  are in a pair.

This is a group of two 🍒.

Skip Count by 2, Now Can You?

2 mittens hang
above the floor.
Then Skippy adds
4 more.

When I skip count,
I count every other number.

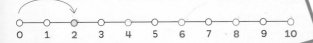

0 1 2 3 4 5 6 7 8 9 10

Skippy decides he wants another pair. Adding 2 more would only be fair!

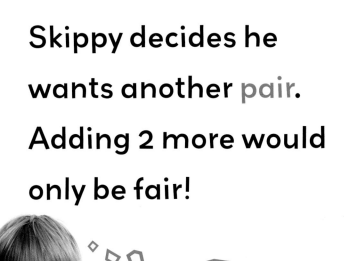

Skippy declares,

"I love to skip count

to find the total amount!"

0 1 2 3 4 5 6 7 8 9 10

Skip Count
by 2
Every Day!

In order to skip count my money, I group my pennies into twos. Then I count 2 for each group I have.

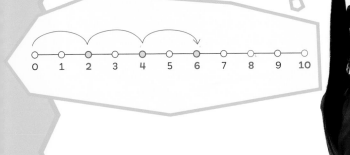

When I fold my laundry,
I group my socks into
pairs of 2.

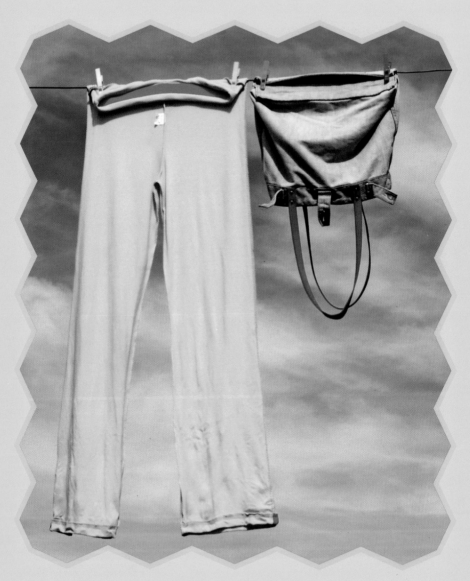

twenty
20

When we hang our laundry, we use 2 clothespins for each item. I can skip count to find how many clothespins are on the line.

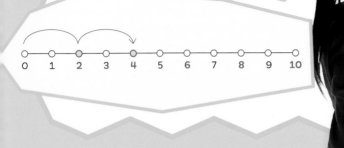

Skip count **by 2 to find** the total **number of** wheels you see.

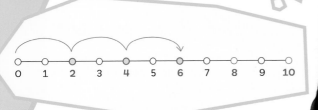

Glossary

clothespin – a clamp used to fasten laundry to a clothesline.

declare – to say something strongly and firmly.

laundry – clothes that have been or are being washed.

money – coins and bills that are issued by a government and can be used to buy things.

penny – a unit of money that is worth one cent.